Picture the Past

Life on a
SOUTHERN
PLANTATION

Sally Senzell Isaacs

Heinemann Library
Chicago, Illinois

© 2001 Reed Educational & Professional Publishing
Published by Heinemann Library,
an imprint of Reed Educational & Professional Publishing,
Chicago, Illinois

Customer Service 888-454-2279
Visit our website at www.heinemannlibrary.com

Produced for Heinemann Library by
    Bender Richardson White.
Editor: Lionel Bender
Designer: Ben White
Picture Researcher: Cathy Stastny
Media Conversion and Typesetting: MW Graphics
Production Controller: Kim Richardson

04 03 02 01
10 9 8 7 6 5 4 3 2 1

Printed in Hong Kong

Library of Congress Cataloging-in-Publication Data.
Isaacs, Sally Senzell, 1950–
    Life on a southern plantation / Sally Senzell Isaacs.
        p. cm. – (Picture the past)
    Includes bibliographical references and index.

        ISBN 1-57572-316-6

1. Plantation life-Mississippi-History-19th century-
Juvenile literature. 2. Mississippi-Social life and customs-
19th century-Juvenile literature. 3. Slaves-Mississippi-
Social conditions-19th century-Juvenile literature.
4. Southern states-Social life and customs-1775-1865-
Juvenile literature. (1. Plantation life-Southern states-
History-19th century. 2. Southern states-Social life and
customs. 3. Slavery.) I. Title.

F341.3.I83 2000
976.2'05-dc21
                                    00-020644

Special thanks to Mike Carpenter, Scott Westerfield, and
Tristan Boyer Binns at Heinemann Library for editorial and
design guidance and direction.

Acknowledgments
The producers and publishers are grateful to the
following for permission to reproduce copyright material:
The Bridgeman Art Library: Christie's Images/Private
Collection, page 26; Louisiana State Museum, Louisiana,
page 7. Corbis Images: Corbis, pages 21, 28; Robert
Holmes, page 11; Minnesota Historical Society, page 23.
Mary Evans Picture Library, page 19. Hulton Getty Picture
Collection, page 30. Peter Newark's American Pictures,
pages 1, 3, 8, 10, 13, 14, 15, 16, 17, 18, 20, 24, 25.
Cover photograph: Corbis Images.

Every effort has been made to contact copyright holders
of any material reproduced in this book. Omissions will
be rectified in subsequent printings if notice is given to
the publisher.

Illustrations by James Field, pages 4, 29; John James,
pages 6, 9, 12, 16.
Map by Stefan Chabluk.
Cover make-up: Mike Pilley, Pelican Graphics.

Note to the Reader
Some words are shown in bold, **like this**.
You can find out what they mean by looking in the
glossary.

ABOUT THIS BOOK
This book tells about daily life
on a cotton plantation in the
Southern United States. The
time period is about 1850 to
1860. There were plantations
throughout the southern states.
Many grew cotton. Others
grew tobacco, rice, or sugar.
We have illustrated the book
with paintings, drawings, and
photographs from plantation
times. We also include artists'
ideas of how things looked on
plantations.

The Consultant
Diane Smolinski has years of experience
interpreting standards documents and
putting them into practice in fourth and
fifth grade classrooms.

The Author
Sally Senzell Isaacs is a professional writer
and editor of nonfiction books for children.
She graduated from Indiana University,
earning a B.S. degree in Education with
majors in American History and Sociology.
For some years, she was the Editorial
Director of Reader's Digest Educational
Division. Sally Senzell Isaacs lives in New
Jersey with her husband and two children.

CONTENTS

Planters and Slaves

Plantation owners were called **planters**. They were rich and lived in large houses. They and their wives wore fancy clothes and gave huge, colorful parties. Their children were well-dressed and well-educated.

Slaves also lived on plantations. They lived in small wooden cabins and worked from sunrise to sunset. Slaves belonged to the planter. He bought the slaves the same way he bought a horse or a plow. Until 1865, slavery was allowed in the United States.

Look for these
The illustration of a plantation boy and girl shows you the subject of each double-page story in the book.

The illustration of cotton-pickers highlights panels with facts and figures about daily life on a southern plantation.

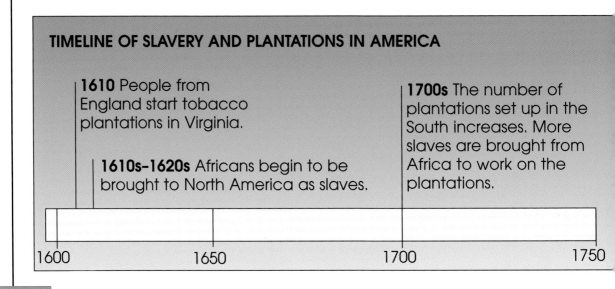

TIMELINE OF SLAVERY AND PLANTATIONS IN AMERICA

1610 People from England start tobacco plantations in Virginia.

1610s–1620s Africans begin to be brought to North America as slaves.

1700s The number of plantations set up in the South increases. More slaves are brought from Africa to work on the plantations.

| 1600 | 1650 | 1700 | 1750 |

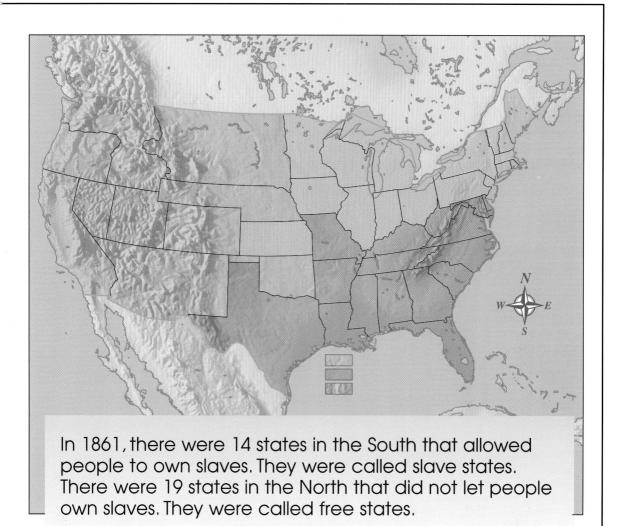

In 1861, there were 14 states in the South that allowed people to own slaves. They were called slave states. There were 19 states in the North that did not let people own slaves. They were called free states.

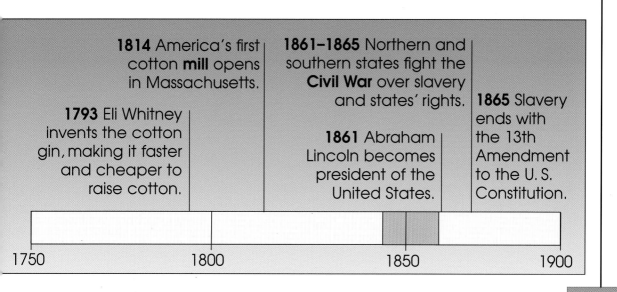

1814 America's first cotton **mill** opens in Massachusetts.

1793 Eli Whitney invents the cotton gin, making it faster and cheaper to raise cotton.

1861–1865 Northern and southern states fight the **Civil War** over slavery and states' rights.

1861 Abraham Lincoln becomes president of the United States.

1865 Slavery ends with the 13th Amendment to the U. S. Constitution.

1750   1800   1850   1900

The Plantation

A plantation had many fields that grew a **crop** such as cotton. It took many people to pick the cotton. After it was picked, the cotton was packed up and shipped to cloth **factories** in Europe or the northern states.

The plantation owner, his family, and his assistants lived in houses. The **slaves** lived in small cabins near the fields.

A large plantation was also like a town. There were many buildings. Sometimes there was a church, a cemetery, and a school. There was an office and a stable for the animals. Some plantations had blacksmith, shoemaker, and carpenter's shops.

Plantation owners were proud of their beautiful homes. When an owner died, he passed the plantation to his oldest son to carry on the family business.

SMALL AND BIG FARMS

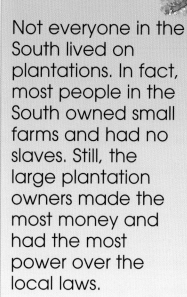

Not everyone in the South lived on plantations. In fact, most people in the South owned small farms and had no slaves. Still, the large plantation owners made the most money and had the most power over the local laws.

Slaves

Planters became rich because they owned **slaves**. A slave is a person who is owned by another person. Some plantations had over 100 slaves. Most slaves worked in the fields. Some worked in the planter's house. Slaves received no money for their work. The planter gave the slaves a small place to live, some food, and some clothes.

AUCTION PRICES

At a slave auction, plantation owners paid about $1,000 (about $30,000 at today's prices) for a strong, skilled slave.

This poster advertises slaves for sale. Slave-hunters kidnapped people in Africa and shipped them to America to sell.

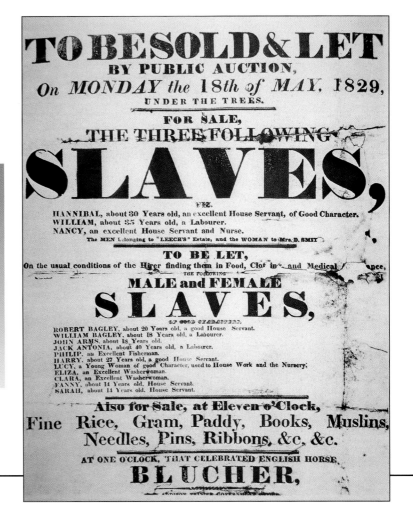

TO BE SOLD & LET
BY PUBLIC AUCTION,
On MONDAY the 18th of MAY, 1829,
UNDER THE TREES.
FOR SALE,
THE THREE FOLLOWING
SLAVES,
VIZ.
HANNIBAL, about 30 Years old, an excellent House Servant, of Good Character.
WILLIAM, about 35 Years old, a Labourer.
NANCY, an excellent House Servant and Nurse.
The MEN belonging to "LEECH'S" Estate, and the WOMAN to Mrs. D. SMIT
TO BE LET,
On the usual conditions of the Hirer finding them in Food, Clothing and Medical ance,
THE FOLLOWING
MALE and FEMALE
SLAVES,
OF GOOD CHARACTERS,
ROBERT BAGLEY, about 20 Years old, a good House Servant.
WILLIAM BAGLEY, about 18 Years old, a Labourer.
JOHN ARMS, about 18 Years old.
JACK ANTONIA, about 40 Years old, a Labourer.
PHILIP, an Excellent Fisherman.
HARRY, about 27 Years old, a good House Servant.
LUCY, a Young Woman of good Character, used to House Work and the Nursery.
ELIZA, an Excellent Washerwoman.
CLARA, an Excellent Washerwoman.
FANNY, about 14 Years old, House Servant.
SARAH, about 14 Years old, House Servant.
Also for Sale, at Eleven o'Clock,
Fine Rice, Gram, Paddy, Books, Muslins,
Needles, Pins, Ribbons, &c. &c.
AT ONE O'CLOCK, THAT CELEBRATED ENGLISH HORSE
BLUCHER,

Slaves could not leave the plantation without a written pass from their owner. Many slave owners were kind to their slaves. Others whipped their slaves and treated them badly.

At a mid-18th century slave auction, a planter is selling some of his slaves. The husband and wife may be sold to different plantations. The baby will stay with its mother.

SLAVES

TO BE SOLD

The Big House

The **planter's** house was called the Big House. It had many fancy rooms. The family entertained guests in the dining room and **parlor**. Large windows let the breeze flow through the house. Summers were hot and there were no electric fans or air conditioners.

This is a Big House on a plantation in the South. When the family wanted to go someplace, a horse and **carriage** pulled up to the front door.

The planter and his wife had a very comfortable bedroom. In the morning, **servants** put warm water in the pitcher for washing and shaving.

The kitchen was outside the Big House. This kept the cooking smells and heat away from the family. Also, if there was a cooking fire, the house was not damaged. There was no running water in the house.

CHAMBER POTS

The toilet was outside the Big House. People kept chamber pots in the bedroom. They used the pots at night. Servants emptied them in the outdoor toilet the next morning.

The Slave Cabins

Most **slaves** lived in rows of cabins by the fields. Sometimes ten people shared one small cabin. Some slaves worked in the Big House. They lived in the house, sometimes in the **attic**. These house **servants** were more comfortable than the field slaves. But they missed living with their friends.

Slaves grew vegetables outside their cabins. They raised chickens and hogs to provide more food than the **planter** gave them.

After a long, back-breaking day in the fields, the slaves came back to their cabins to cook, clean, and wash clothes.

The slaves were like family to each other. They tried to cheer each other up with songs and prayers. They did not want their children to forget the customs of their homeland, Africa. They told stories about the old country and played African games.

Work in the Fields

On a small plantation, the **planter** and his family worked with the **slaves**. On a large plantation, the planter worked in an office. From there he made decisions about selling his **crops**. He gave orders to an **overseer** who watched the slaves work in the fields.

The slaves brought in cotton from the fields. If they had not picked enough, the overseer might whip them.

A SLAVE'S DAY

5:00 A.M. Wake up to the sound of a bell or horn. Eat a quick breakfast. Pack a lunch. Run to the fields to work.
NOON: Eat lunch quickly.
8:00 P.M. Come home from the fields. Eat dinner. Take care of the cabin and garden. Go to sleep.

The overseer made sure the slaves worked hard. Men, women, and children spent all day in the fields. In the spring, they plowed the fields then planted seeds. In the summer, they pulled weeds. In the fall, they started picking the cotton. The plants produced cotton for several months. In between all this, there were fences to repair and ditches to dig.

From time to time, the planter and his wife would inspect the plantation to check that work was going well.

Work in the House

Every morning, the **planter's** wife told the house **servants** what to do. Each job took more time than it does today. Everything had to be done by hand. There were no machines to make work easy. A cook churned the butter for the family breakfast. A maid hung the rugs over a rope and beat out the dust. Another servant built the cooking fire and filled the oil lamps.

The laundry maids spent hours washing clothes. They washed them in tubs of water. To wash a fancy dress, they first had to remove all the buttons and lace.

WASHING DISHES

How the maids washed dishes:
1. Take the dishes to the yard.
2. Make a fire. Heat a large pot of water.
3. Pour warm water into two barrels.
4. In one barrel, wash the dishes with home-made soap.
5. Rinse the dishes in the other barrel.

Some plantations had more than twelve **slaves** working around the house.

The planter's wife spent hours at her writing desk. She sent letters to her family and friends in other cities. She shared news about births, deaths, and special parties coming up. Planning parties was another important job of the planter's wife.

Planters' Children

It was important for the **planters'** children to act like ladies and gentlemen. Boys closely watched their fathers run the plantation. Girls took lessons in drawing, sewing, and music. Girls were asked to sing or play piano for the house guests.

The planter's children and slave children often played together. They explored in the woods, fished in the pond, or played games.

Many boys wanted to become plantation owners like their fathers. Others wanted to be army officers, lawyers, or doctors. Most girls dreamed of getting married and making a lovely home for their husbands and children. Some girls hoped to help people in churches and hospitals.

Usually, one of the servants was in charge of the planter's children. She made sure they dressed neatly and studied their lessons.

Slave Children

Servants did not work on Sunday. Every Saturday night, they met outside the Big House. They sang, danced, and told African stories.

The very young **slave** children were allowed to run and play around the plantation. But by age eight or nine, they had to work in the fields. The smallest children picked insects off the **crops** or pulled weeds. Some carried water buckets to the other workers.

Slave children worried about their future. Would they spend all their lives as slaves? They heard stories about slaves who ran away to northern states where slavery was not allowed. Some white people were helping slaves escape. But others were catching run-away slaves and punishing them.

Slave parents taught their children to work hard and act nicely to white people. That way they could avoid punishments.

Going to School

Slave children did not go to school. In fact, many states had laws against teaching slaves to read and write. Sometimes a preacher or kind member of the **planter's** family taught some slaves to read. But the slaves had no money to buy books.

SCHOOL LESSONS

- Reading the Bible
- Good Manners
- American History
- Oceans and Continents of the World
- Arithmetic
- Handwriting

Children picking cotton on a Southern plantation. The children work in the fields alongside their parents and other adult slaves.

The planters' children walked or rode horses to school. A slave went with them to carry the books. By age twelve, many girls stopped going to school. They still took lessons in music and French. Boys went to school longer than girls.

Many planters' sons left home to live at military school. They learned to become officers in the army.

Planters' Clothes

Many **planters** bought new clothes from city stores. Men and boys wore a shirt, wool pants, a jacket, and boots. Men often tied a cravat, or scarf, around their necks. Beneath it all, they wore long underwear.

People always seemed to look "dressed up."

A tiny waist was in style. Women laced **corsets** under their dresses to pinch in their waists.

From the time they were about six years old, many girls fussed over their hair and clothing. **Servants** spent hours getting them ready for parties. Their dresses laced up tightly at the waist and puffed out at the bottom.

Slaves' Clothes

The house **servants** were supposed to look neat and proper. Those **slaves** often wore clothes that the **planter's** family did not want anymore. The field slaves did not dress as well. Each man received one or two sets of clothing a year. The women received cloth and thread to make their own clothes.

This family of parents and children were born on the plantation. They wore the same clothes for days at a time. The mother made clothes for the children.

Field slaves wore loose-fitting clothes so they could move easily.

In the fields, men wore shirts and pants and often a hat. Women wore long skirts and blouses and a headscarf. Everyone received one pair of leather shoes a year. When the shoes wore out, the slaves patched them with rags. Some slave children wore long cotton shirts. They often had no pants or shoes.

Food

Several **servants** worked in the kitchen to make meals for the **planter's** family. Most food was cooked in iron pots on an open fire.

Each week the planter gave the **slaves** some corn and bacon. To add to this, slaves grew vegetables in their gardens, fished, and trapped wild animals.

The planter's family ate their biggest meal at noon. It might include pork chops, rice and crayfish, corn bread, sweet potato pie, and lemonade. The meal was served by servants.

Plantation Recipe—Sweet Potato Pie

Sweet potatoes grow well in the South. They grow under the ground. In the 1860s, sweet potato pie was baked in front of the kitchen fireplace. Follow the instructions below to make the pie as people did on southern plantations about 150 years ago.

WARNING: Do not cook anything unless there is an adult to help you. Always ask an adult to use the knives, the oven, and to handle hot food.

YOU WILL NEED
1 40-ounce ($1\frac{1}{4}$-kg) can sweet potatoes
3 eggs
1 cup (240 ml) milk
$\frac{1}{2}$ cup (120 g) sugar
1 cup (240 g) brown sugar
3 tablespoons butter, melted
$\frac{1}{2}$ teaspoon salt
1 teaspoon cinnamon
$\frac{1}{2}$ teaspoon nutmeg
1 deep-dish pie crust or 2 regular 9-inch (23-cm) pie crusts

FOLLOW THE STEPS

1. Preheat the oven to 450 degrees Fahrenheit (230 degrees Centigrade).
2. Mash the sweet potatoes until they are smooth.
3. Beat the eggs. Add the milk, sugar, brown sugar, melted butter, salt, cinnamon, and nutmeg.
4. Pour the egg mixture into the sweet potatoes. Mix well.
5. Pour the mixture into the pie crust(s). Bake at 450 degrees Fahrenheit (230 degrees Centigrade) for 10 minutes. Then turn the heat down to 350 degrees Fahrenheit (180 degrees Centigrade) and bake for 50 minutes. To tell if the pie is done, stick a knife into the pie. It should come out clean.

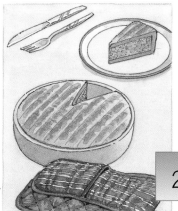

The End of Slavery

The **Civil War** between northern and southern states started in 1861. **Planters** and their sons left to fight the war. Women ran the plantations for as long as possible. Northern soldiers took over many planters' homes. Some camped out there. Others stole food, animals, and jewelry. Many plantations were burned to the ground by northern soldiers.

In 1865, the war ended. That year, all the **slaves** were freed. Many stayed to rebuild the plantations. They worked for money or for a piece of land. They were now able to build schools—like this one—and buy books for their children.

Glossary

attic space at the top of a house, under the roof

blacksmith someone who makes things from iron, such as horseshoes

carriage something used to carry people and goods, pulled by horses

Civil War in the United States, a war between people of the northern and southern states. The war lasted from 1861 to 1865. The South wanted to let new states have the right to own slaves. The North did not want slavery.

corset women's underwear that fits tightly at the waist

crops plants grown to provide food or products to sell

factory building where things are made by machine

mill factory where such products as cloth and steel are made

overseer person on a plantation who is in charge of the slaves

parlor room in an old house, similar to a living room, where people sit with their guests

plantation large farm on which one main crop is grown

planter owner of a large plantation

preacher someone who leads church services

servant someone who works in another person's house, usually cooking, cleaning, and serving

slave someone who is owned by another person and is made to work for that person

More Books to Read

Bial, Raymond. *The Strength of These Arms: Life in the Slave Quarters.* New York: Houghton Mifflin Company, 1997.
Stone, Lynn M. *Plantations.* Vero Beach, Fla.: Rourke Publications, 1999.

Index